IMAGES
of Rail

CENTRAL ILLINOIS
TRAIN DEPOTS

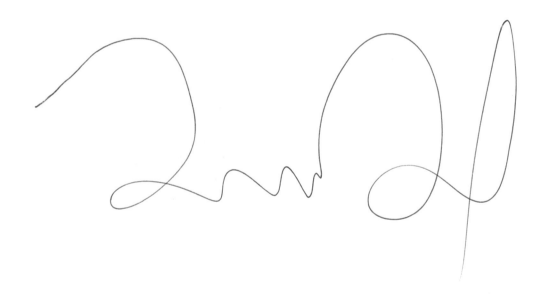

IMAGES
of Rail

CENTRAL ILLINOIS
TRAIN DEPOTS

Thomas Dyrek
Introduction by Jack Keefe

ARCADIA
PUBLISHING

Copyright © 2021 by Thomas Dyrek
ISBN 978-1-4671-0605-4

Published by Arcadia Publishing
Charleston, South Carolina

Printed in the United States of America

Library of Congress Control Number: 2020945339

For all general information, please contact Arcadia Publishing:
Telephone 843-853-2070
Fax 843-853-0044
E-mail sales@arcadiapublishing.com
For customer service and orders:
Toll-Free 1-888-313-2665

Visit us on the Internet at www.arcadiapublishing.com

*Dedicated to my grandmother Susie Pope for getting
me interested in writing and for driving through a
cornfield so I could take a picture for this book*

CONTENTS

ACKNOWLEDGMENTS

As a teenage railroad photographer who was interested in getting the "perfect shot" of modern trains passing through town, old railroad stations were the last thing on my mind. Although I was largely uninterested in the history of railroads, one afternoon that all changed forever. While exploring a local railroad on Google Earth, I found an old station that, to my surprise, was still standing long after the last passenger train had roared through. Wondering if it would make a good backdrop for a future train photograph, my grandma and I drove down to see it, and after taking a few pictures, I was hooked. Over the next few years, I traveled all over Illinois and the surrounding states to photograph these fascinating old structures and research their history to learn about the stories they have to tell. Along the way, I became acquainted with several other railroad history fans and "depotologists," as I like to call them, and my interest in railroading expanded from taking pictures of an Amtrak train to writing several articles about the history of what was—and still is—the backbone of America.

This book is a great way for me to share the stories I have discovered with other curious railfans, history buffs, and simply those who want to recall memories (or make new ones) through these historic buildings. I would like to thank my friend and mentor Jack Keefe for writing the introduction and sharing his knowledge and several vintage photographs, the McLean County Museum of History, Steve Smedley, Roger Holmes, Dale Jenkins, Ryan Tidaback, Tyler Scott, Isaiah Bradford, Dave Gentry, Nick Goedecke and the Chatham Railroad Museum for sharing photographs, Caroline Anderson at Arcadia Publishing for helping me work on this project, and my friends and family for their support and for taking me on countless "depot hunting" trips. Without these people, this book would not have been possible.

Unless otherwise noted, all images appear courtesy of the author.

INTRODUCTION

There always has been something about a railroad station. Even to an uninterested observer, it can spark a little bit of interest. For example, what are those mounted lights for? What goes on in there? Why do some towns have these trackside buildings while some do not?

Rural and city railroad stations or depots have been around for as long as there have been railroads in the United States. Plenty happens at these stations—all of it designed to keep business thriving, passengers riding, and trains safely rolling along any particular depot's little stretch of railroad.

Almost every city, town, and whistle-stop had a depot in the late 19th century. Residents of places without a depot schemed and lobbied their local railroad to get one. If a location had no depot, its growth could be stunted or outright doomed. Residents of depot-less towns and hamlets had to travel by horse and buggy to the nearest station-blessed town before they could board a train unless they lived at a flag stop, at which they could "flag" a train, waving it to a stop so that it could take on passengers.

Two stories come to mind. At Hendrix, neighbors pressed the Illinois Central for a depot and finally got one in the 1880s. To celebrate, the locals threw a potluck dinner at the station on New Year's Day. Alas, the depot was eventually closed and moved to Kerrick. However, the Hendrix elevator endured for decades after the closure. At Yuton, neighbors also agitated for a depot, but the Lake Erie & Western instead put up a passenger shelter; these were three-sided structures with the fourth side exposed to wind, rain, and snow. Imagine the passengers-in-waiting getting cold and wet as they wondered why their train was late. Yuton's grain elevator is still there, but the shelter is long gone.

A small-town railroad station was generally staffed by one or two people. There was an operator, whose duty was to copy and deliver the train orders dictated by a faraway dispatcher over a telephone or telegraph wire, and an agent, who would sell tickets and deal with local shippers. Of course, if there was only one person assigned to work the depot, he or she had to do both jobs.

Outside the station, a sign marked the location of the town, elevator, or junction as it appeared on the railroad timetable. Sometimes, a passenger platform was part of the site. Lights and signal boards were used to inform crews of approaching trains and if there were train orders to pick up.

Much bigger operations could be found in larger cities and towns where railroad lines crossed or trains changed crews. Sometimes, division offices hummed with activity all their own just upstairs from the passengers' waiting room.

The city stations were often made of brick or stone and were multiple-story affairs instead of the single-story wood-frame structures of the small towns. The Illinois Central depots at Clinton or Amboy were good examples, as were the Wabash Station at Decatur and the Bloomington Union Station of 1913.

A busy city depot often offered extra services to the traveling public. Coffee shops and newsstands were not uncommon. In some stations, shoeshine boys and men were available and ready to polish a traveler's shoes.

In their heyday, local railroad stations were places of business, witnesses to tearful goodbyes and joyous reunions, somewhere to ship milk in the wee hours of the morning, or where one could get the very first copy of the morning paper from the county seat. They bustled with the electric air that promises places to go, things to do, and people to see.

This crescendo built until World War I. Military conflicts have a way of accelerating technology, and this war was no different. The demands of war led to the proliferation of motor vehicles in the military. The world was already shrinking when the conflict began; internal combustion engines were already making highway travel—and shipping—more lucrative. The first motor car appeared in Bloomington in 1901. It belonged to a locomotive engineer, of all people. By the next decade, fire departments had motorized vehicles, motorcycle cops appeared on city streets, and motorized farm implements began taking hold in the fields.

By the time the war ended in 1918, words like "truck" and "bus" were as common as "car." The phrase "horseless carriage" was becoming as outmoded as the horse and buggy itself. Almost everyone had wheels of some kind. The impact of motor vehicles on the railroads was light at first, but in the years after World War I, it became obvious that cars and trucks were cutting into the railroads' freight and passenger revenues. People drove their cars from town to town instead of taking the train; shippers turned to trucks for more customer-friendly schedules. In the 1930s, the Great Depression slowed everything down, but the damage to the railroads had been done.

As a result, passenger trains were shorter in length and eventually dropped, freight service dwindled, some branch lines were abandoned, and many depots closed. The wartime traffic of the 1940s provided a brief reprieve. But despite the dieselization of the 1940s and 1950s (and because of government regulations of the time), the decline resumed after 1945.

There were other factors that led to the decline of the railroad station. The advent of centralized traffic control (CTC) reduced the need for trackside operators, placing the control of trains in the hands of dispatchers. Poor rail service, the encroachment of trucking, and the railroads' emphasis on long-haul service deflated local shipping profits. And if there was no need for the depots, railroads chose to demolish them rather than pay property taxes on them.

Fast-forward to the 21st century: Most of the small-town depots are gone, along with many of their big-city counterparts. Amtrak has taken over some of the stations and even built some new ones, but sadly, the quaint railroad days of the mid-20th century are gone.

There is still history to record. Some depots escaped the wrecker's ball or the vandal's torch. Some sit derelict and rotting, most of them removed from their trackside locations. Others have new life—look for these buildings repurposed as restaurants, antique stores, hobby shops, public libraries, and even police stations.

In this book, author Thomas Dyrek has assembled his own work and that of others to reintroduce us to the railroad stations of Central Illinois. It is a substantial undertaking with results likely to show many readers their hometown depots one more time, if not for the very first time. No work of this sort can ever be complete, but this book is significant as a beginning and deserves a serious look. Enjoy.

—Jack Keefe

One

Depots of the Toledo, Peoria & Western

This early-1900s postcard shows the Toledo, Peoria & Western (TP&W) depot at Fairbury, which was built in 1904. This is one of just a handful of station buildings on the TP&W that were constructed of brick. For a time, this depot was also shared with the Wabash Railroad. It was torn down in 1934, and the bricks were used to construct a new church in Fairbury.

Although the 1904 Fairbury depot was torn down, the Toledo, Peoria & Western (TP&W) still needed an active station in Fairbury to handle freight and mail along with the occasional ticket sales for passengers, who were able to ride in a caboose on freight trains for years after regular passenger trains had been discontinued. This small metal depot was built in 1963 to serve these purposes. (Photograph by Jack Keefe.)

One of the Toledo, Peoria & Western's early wood-frame depots stood in Gridley. The town of Gridley was named after Ashael Gridley, a prominent politician in McLean County and a friend of Abraham Lincoln. This 1965 photograph shows the depot, which was built in 1876, about a decade before it was torn down. (Photograph by Jack Keefe.)

Two

DEPOTS OF THE ALTON ROUTE

The Chicago & Alton (C&A) Railroad had many beautiful stations in Central Illinois. This one was located at Dwight. Built in 1891, the Dwight depot was the only station on the railroad with this design. This depot remained in active service until 2017, when it was replaced with a modern Amtrak station. (Photograph by Jack Keefe.)

Odell is the next town south of Dwight on the Alton Route. This handsome wood-frame depot was built in the late 1800s and remained standing into the 1970s. This 1960s photograph shows a southbound Gulf, Mobile & Ohio (GM&O) passenger train at the Odell depot. In 1947, the Chicago & Alton was merged into the GM&O. (Photograph by Roger A. Holmes.)

South of Odell is the small hamlet of Cayuga, where this long-abandoned Alton station stands. Originally located at Pontiac, this building likely dates to the railroad's construction in 1853. In 1913, it was relocated to Cayuga to make way for a new station in Pontiac. After it was closed sometime during World War II, the building was turned 90 degrees and moved to the nearby grain elevator to be used as an office.

Interestingly, the newer Pontiac depot (mentioned in the previous caption) also still stands today, although it is in much better shape than Cayuga's. As Pontiac grew, the need for a larger depot increased, hence the 1913 construction of this building. As in Dwight, this station was used well into the Amtrak era until it was also replaced in 2017 with a new station. (Courtesy of the Chatham Railroad Museum.)

Moving south from Pontiac along the Chicago & Alton, one will find the town of Lexington, where this depot, built in 1888, still stands. The Chicago & Alton had a few depots with this type of classic Victorian-era design. In the early 1980s, the Lexington depot was saved from demolition and moved to a site on Main Street in downtown Lexington, where it has been restored and currently houses a business.

The Chicago & Alton depot at Towanda was built around 1910 to replace an earlier structure that likely dated to the railroad's construction in 1853. After it had been in service for about 50 years, the Towanda station was unceremoniously razed in the 1970s despite community efforts to save it. An almost identical station also stood at Atlanta, but it too was razed in the 1970s. (Photograph by Jack Keefe.)

Bloomington was home of the Chicago & Alton's main shop facilities. Known locally as the "C&A Shops," the facility consisted of 12 buildings used for building, repairing, and maintaining the railroad's equipment. This was the Bloomington Freight Depot, which was used for shipping and storing goods. The C&A Shops were once the largest employer in Bloomington. The shops employed over 2,000 men at their peak in the first half of the 20th century.

Despite declining rail traffic, the Chicago & Alton shops survived several company mergers that took place on the former C&A property and remained in service into the late 1980s. This 1975 photograph shows a Gulf, Mobile & Ohio locomotive parked next to one of the shop buildings. Unfortunately, all of the shop buildings except the freight depot have been razed, and the once-bustling complex is now an overgrown field. (Photograph by Robert Stevens.)

Shirley, Illinois, is a small village located on the southern outskirts of Bloomington-Normal. In 1900, the Chicago & Alton dug a cut through the center of town for the tracks to pass through to avoid a steep grade north of town. In 1902, this station was built at the top of the Shirley Cut, with steps leading down to the platform and tracks. (Photograph by Jack Keefe.)

The McLean depot is said to be one of the oldest still standing in the state and the only surviving depot in Illinois to have been passed by Abraham Lincoln's 1865 funeral train. Dating to the construction of the Chicago & Alton in 1853 and 1854, the depot was extensively remodeled in 1926. After the remodeling was completed, William Hilligoss became the new agent. Hilligoss served as the McLean agent for 44 years before retiring in December 1970, when the depot was closed. In the following weeks, the depot was threatened with demolition, but two local history buffs were able to save and relocate it to a site near Route 66 for use as a business. This 1963 photograph shows the depot in its final years of service. Today, the McLean depot is home to a model railroad store. (Photograph by Jack Keefe.)

A Gulf, Mobile & Ohio passenger train is passing by the Atlanta depot in this 1960s photograph. Atlanta was located at a junction between the Chicago & Alton and the Pennsylvania Railroad; however, both railroads had their own depots in town instead of sharing a single building. Like the Towanda depot, this building was demolished in the early 1970s. (Photograph by Roger A. Holmes.)

This photograph shows the Lincoln depot during the time the Gulf, Mobile & Ohio owned the Alton Route. Lincoln is the only town that was named after Abraham Lincoln when he was still living. Just behind the photographer was a freight depot, and down the tracks was a junction with the Illinois Central. This depot is still used by Amtrak. (Courtesy of the Chatham Railroad Museum.)

The small village of Broadwell, south of Lincoln, almost lost its Alton depot to a nasty derailment. On November 16, 1945, northbound passenger train No. 6 hit a truck at a nearby crossing. The force of the crash derailed the engine and 11 cars on the train. The depot was not affected by the derailment, but the agent was very shaken up. (Photograph by Jack Keefe.)

Just south of Broadwell is Elkhart, where this early 1900s depot stood. This 1970s photograph shows the depot in its final years. The agency closed shortly after this was taken, and the building stood abandoned for several years before being torn down prior to 1980. Today, no evidence remains of a depot. (Courtesy of the Chatham Railroad Museum.)

The Williamsville depot was built around 1900. This 1960s photograph shows a southbound Gulf, Mobile & Ohio passenger train passing during the depot's final years of service with the railroad. The town of Williamsville was able to save the depot from demolition and turn it into a library in the 1970s. (Courtesy of the Chatham Railroad Museum.)

Constructed in 1895, the depot at Springfield is still open today. During the 1960s, passenger trains were struggling to compete with automobiles and planes in the United States. Many railroads stopped passenger operations, but thanks to this line being the most direct route from Chicago to St. Louis, its passenger operations survived, and today, Amtrak runs 10 trains per day down the Alton Route.

The Chatham depot was built in 1902 to replace an earlier structure that was destroyed by a fire. While the remains were still smoldering, construction of the current depot began across the street. Since the depot was taken out of service in 1972, it has been involved in a handful of uses. Today, it is home to the Chatham Railroad Museum, which supplied several images for this book.

Moving back toward the north, one will find the village of Greenview. Located on the Chicago & Alton's Bloomington-to-Jacksonville branch line, the Greenview depot survived the early 1980s abandonment of the railroad between Bloomington and Jacksonville. Sometime later, it was relocated to a private residence and has since been restored and converted for use as a storage shed.

Petersburg was the next stop south of Greenview on the Jacksonville Line. Petersburg's Chicago & Alton depot was built in 1887. After years of disrepair, a one-man preservation attempt, and extensive remodeling that turned it into a home, the Petersburg depot was damaged by a suspected arson fire in 2007, and the remains were demolished soon after.

Located southeast of Petersburg is Talulla, where another Jacksonville Line depot has been preserved and repurposed. Built around 1910, the structure was repurposed as a bank after the depot closed. Prior to World War II, most depots were built with a bay window, as shown here. These windows allowed the agent to look both ways down the tracks to watch for approaching trains. (Courtesy of the Chatham Railroad Museum.)

Another of the Chicago & Alton's branch lines was the Dwight Branch, which ran from the mainline in Dwight to Lacon on the Illinois River. This photograph shows the depot at Metamora with a freight train passing by. The Metamora depot was built around 1900, and after it was closed in the 1970s, a local farmer purchased it for use as a storage shed on his farm. The building was dismantled and moved to his property outside of town, but the pieces were never reassembled. Those pieces are reportedly still in storage on the farm, and today, local railroad and history buffs are working on tracking them down. (Photograph by Roger A. Holmes.)

Three

DEPOTS OF PEORIA

4703. Union Depot, Peoria, Ill.

Known as the River City, Peoria was once a major rail hub with over 10 railroads serving the area at its peak during the first half of the 20th century. Peoria Union Station was where many of these railroads terminated. Opened in 1882, this unique structure saw its last train in 1955. Sadly, Union Station was destroyed in a fire a few years later.

Unlike Union Station, Peoria's Rock Island depot survives today. Built in 1899, the depot was replaced by a new structure in 1967, but the old one was saved and repurposed. Today, it is home to a bar and restaurant. The tracks in front of the depot are owned by the Iowa Interstate Railroad.

The 1967 replacement Rock Island depot is also still standing. Located north of the downtown area, this station was built adjacent to the Rock Island's yard and locomotive facilities in Peoria. Today, the yard is no more; nor is the Rock Island, which shut down on March 31, 1980, after years of bankruptcy. The City of Peoria currently uses the building for storage. This photograph shows the sign on the side of the depot.

The Chillicothe depot was built in 1889. This was a common design for Rock Island depots, and another example once stood at nearby Henry. After years of sitting vacant and falling into disrepair, the depot was lovingly restored by the Chillicothe Historical Society in the 1980s, and it now houses a railroad museum.

This photograph shows the Rock Island's special bicentennial diesel engine passing the Chillicothe depot after it had been vacated and boarded up. To celebrate the nation's bicentennial in 1976, many U.S. railroads painted locomotives with a special red, white and blue paint scheme, and the Rock Island participated by painting locomotive No. 652. (Photograph by Steve Smedley.)

One of the major railroads that served the Peoria area was the Minneapolis & St. Louis (M&StL). Contrary to its name, the M&StL never reached St. Louis, with Peoria being the southernmost point on the railroad. This photograph shows a maintenance shed along the tracks in Trivoli, a village west of Peoria. (Photograph by Montague L. Powell.)

In 1960, the Minneapolis & St. Louis was acquired by the Chicago & North Western (C&NW). This photograph from July 1986 shows a C&NW train passing the abandoned M&StL depot at Hanna City. Just a few weeks after this photograph was taken, some local kids set fire to the structure, and it was destroyed. (Photograph by Steve Smedley.)

Another Peoria railroad was the Chicago, Burlington & Quincy (CB&Q), which shared this depot with the Minneapolis & St. Louis at a junction between the two railroads at Farmington, west of Hanna City. Originally, both railroads had their own depots in Farmington, but by the time this photograph was taken in the 1960s, operations for both railroads had been consolidated into this building. Today, both depots are long gone. (Photograph by Roger A. Holmes.)

Unlike most railroad junctions where the tracks crossed each other at the same level, Farmington's junction was an overpass. Both the CB&Q and the Minneapolis & St. Louis were abandoned in the early 2000s, but the bridge that carried the CB&Q over the M&StL survived well into the 21st century, albeit abandoned and in poor shape. This bridge was removed in 2019, but the abutments are still in place.

While Farmington's Chicago, Burlington & Quincy (CB&Q) depot was torn down, the town of Yates City, north of Farmington, was able to preserve its CB&Q depot; shortly before the CB&Q's successor, the Burlington Northern, was set to demolish this structure, it was relocated to a nearby park and restored. This photograph shows a BN train at the Yates City depot before it was moved. (Photograph by Steve Smedley.)

One of the most important types of freight transported by rail in Central Illinois was—and still is—grain. In addition to having depots, most Central Illinois communities had a grain elevator. The Edwards depot on the Chicago, Burlington & Quincy was demolished years ago, but its grain elevator remains. Often, agents in a depot would control train movements to pick up or drop off cars at elevators.

The Chicago & Alton (C&A) Railroad built this depot in Pekin in 1898. Originally located at the corner of Broadway and Fourteenth Street, the building was relocated in 2008 to a nearby park at the site of the Santa Fe Railroad's Pekin shops and cosmetically restored. Today, this is the last known surviving C&A depot in the Peoria area.

Pekin Terminal Station was where trains of the Peoria & Eastern, Peoria & Pekin Union, Chicago & Illinois Midland, Santa Fe, and Peoria Terminal Railroads once stopped. This station was razed prior to World War II. After the station was demolished, all of the railroads that once served it used their own stations in town. This undated postcard shows Pekin Terminal Station in its heyday.

Lewistown's Chicago, Burlington & Quincy depot was built around 1880. It was moved back from the tracks in the 1970s and is currently abandoned. During the 1980s, an annual railroad festival was held nearby, and a model railroad was set up inside the abandoned depot for people to view.

A few blocks from the Lewistown depot is the last remaining structure from the Fulton County Narrow Gauge (FCNG) Railroad. Most railroads' tracks are standard gauge, meaning the rails are four feet, eight and a half inches apart. Narrow-gauge rails are only three feet apart. The FCNG served several communities southwest of Peoria and operated from 1880 to 1930. The Lewistown depot is now home to an FCNG museum.

Four

DEPOTS OF THE ILLINOIS CENTRAL

The Illinois Central (IC) Railroad began operations in 1851. The IC's main route connected Chicago with New Orleans, but it also had many smaller branch lines running throughout Illinois. This is the IC's depot at Ashkum, which was built in 1941 using materials from an older depot that once stood here. In 1998, the Illinois Central was taken over by the Canadian National Railway, which currently operates this part of the line. The Ashkum depot is still standing today, although it is boarded up and derelict.

South of Ashkum is the town of Gilman, where the Illinois Central (IC) crosses the Toledo, Peoria & Western (TP&W). The Gilman depot was built by the IC in 1909, but the TP&W also used it. Gilman is located at a point where an IC branch line splits off from the New Orleans mainline and heads southwest toward Clinton and Springfield.

Farther down the branch line is the town of Melvin, where another World War II–era Illinois Central depot stands. This design was called Type B and was used on many modern depots on the IC at the time. Other examples in the area were at Pontiac, Maroa, and Cooksville. Today, only a handful of Type B buildings are still standing.

Gibson City is located at another junction between the Illinois Central, Wabash, and Lake Erie & Western Railroads. Instead of having a union depot shared by every railroad, each company had its own facilities in town. This is the Illinois Central's station, which was built around 1910. Today, Canadian National owns it and uses it for storage. (Photograph by Jack Keefe.)

The line between Gilman and Springfield was originally built by the Gilman, Clinton & Springfield (GC&S) Railroad, a predecessor to the Illinois Central. The IC gained control of the GC&S in 1877. The original GC&S depot at Bellflower (pictured) was built in 1871. Prior to the depot being located here, Bellflower was spelled "Belleflower." (Photograph by Jack Keefe.)

The Illinois Central depot in Farmer City was located near a junction with the Peoria & Eastern Railway. This was another city where each railroad had its own depot instead of sharing one. Today, both depots are gone, as is the Peoria & Eastern, which was abandoned in 1994 due to a nearby bridge needing heavy repairs that the railroad could not afford. (Photograph by Jack Keefe.)

The Clinton depot was located at a junction with the former Gilman, Clinton & Springfield line and the north–south Gruber Line, one of the Illinois Central's earliest branch lines that connected Freeport with the New Orleans main at Centralia. The depot's upper floors housed offices and a dispatching facility. In 1986, the Clinton depot was razed despite attempts by the community to save it. (Photograph by Jack Keefe.)

An unusually designed Illinois Central depot stood at Kenney, located southwest of Clinton. This depot was shared with the Pennsylvania Railroad, but it was built by the IC. The Pennsylvania line here connected Peoria with Decatur and was abandoned decades ago. However, the IC line is still in service today. (Photograph by Jack Keefe.)

Pontiac's Type B depot was built in January 1943. Pontiac was located on another Illinois Central branch line, and while most of that line was abandoned, a small section that ran past the depot survived for decades, so trains on the nearby Chicago & Alton line could access a paper mill. Union Pacific, current owners of the C&A line, razed this depot in March 2019.

During World War II, many station agents left the railroad to serve in the military. As a result, women and children were temporarily hired to fill agents' roles until the original agents could return home. This 1945 photograph shows 14-year-old Arnold Hering serving as the temporary agent at the Illinois Central depot in Hudson. In 1975, Hudson was making plans to acquire the depot and restore it for use as a library, but it was destroyed in a suspicious fire before any work had begun. Today, little evidence of the railroad remains in Hudson except a small stone culvert over a creek in downtown. (Courtesy of the McLean County Museum of History.)

In 1941, the Illinois Central depot at Kerrick was sold to Charles Thatcher, who moved it to his farm west of Kappa for use as a barn. Interestingly, the farmhouse was built on an old bridge over a creek. Today, the house is gone, but local depot historians have hopes that the Kerrick depot may have been relocated and survives today. (Courtesy of the McLean County Museum of History.)

This 1905 photograph shows the Illinois Central depot at Randolph, a small community between Bloomington and Heyworth. The names of the people in the photograph are unknown, although the man in the suit appears to be the station agent. The bicycle device on the track is called a velocipede—an early vehicle used to inspect tracks for any issues. (Courtesy of Jack Keefe.)

Heyworth is just south of Randolph. An attractive 1880s depot stood here, but by the time this 1963 photograph was taken, it had been replaced by this Type B structure. Shortly after this picture was taken, Heyworth tore down the building without permission from the Illinois Central, which resulted in legal issues. It is unknown, at least to this author, what eventually became of that legal battle. (Photograph by Jack Keefe.)

Decatur was home to multiple large, stunning train stations. This was the Illinois Central's, which was unfortunately demolished in 1951 after passenger service had ended. Today, all that remains of this beautiful structure is the abandoned baggage room, which is the farthest section to the left in this postcard from the early 1900s. Nearby was a junction with the Wabash Railroad, which has a Decatur station that is still standing today.

The Latham Illinois Central depot was built in 1900. This design was used with a handful of other depots on the railroad, but this depot at Latham is the only surviving example. In the 1970s, it was relocated to a town park, where it was restored and now houses a library. This is the only surviving IC depot between Lincoln and Decatur.

Unfortunately, the Mt. Pulaski depot was the subject of another failed preservation attempt in the early 2000s. The depot remained in service as an office and storage facility for Canadian National (CN) long after passenger service ended on this line. In 2003, CN made plans to tear it down. The town made an effort to save and relocate it, but when this fell through, it was razed. (Photograph by Jack Keefe.)

The Illinois Central's depot at Lincoln was repurposed as a home many years ago and has been remodeled to the point where there is nothing left of the depot. However, it is still a popular photograph stop for depot fans. A few hundred feet away was a junction between the IC and Chicago & Alton, but the IC's tracks through this part of Lincoln are now gone.

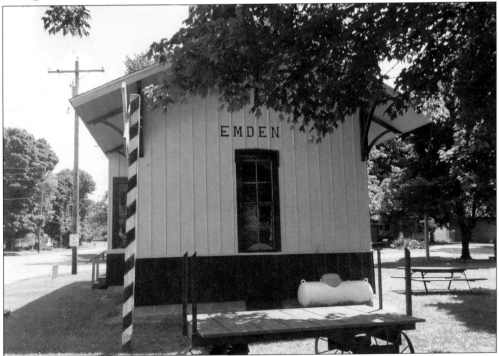

Emden was able to save its Illinois Central depot in the 1970s and move it back from the tracks for preservation. Located about halfway between Lincoln and Peoria, the Emden depot was lovingly restored by the community and turned into a library. This is the only surviving depot on this stretch of the line.

In 1972, the Illinois Central merged with the Gulf, Mobile & Ohio to form Illinois Central Gulf (ICG). The name was changed back to "Illinois Central" in 1988. This 1983 image shows an ICG train passing the abandoned depot at Green Valley shortly before it was torn down. (Photograph by Steve Smedley.)

Moving back along the Chicago–to–New Orleans mainline brings one to the small community of Pesotum, located just south of Champaign-Urbana. This 1990s view of the Illinois Central's Pesotum depot shows the building after it had been closed and abandoned by the railroad. Thankfully, by the end of the decade, the building had been moved back from the tracks and restored. (Photograph by Dave Gentry.)

42

The Illinois Central's Champaign depot was built in 1899 and relocated away from the tracks around 1924, when the tracks through Champaign were elevated. After the move, the depot was modified to become part of the freight operations at the IC's Champaign yard. It is still standing and is currently being used by a business.

After the tracks through Champaign were elevated, a new depot was constructed and remained in service until 1999, when it was replaced by a modern depot across the street. Like the 1899 depot, this depot was turned into a business after its railroad days were over. The 1999 depot is still a stopping point for Amtrak trains.

The Rantoul depot was built around 1920. At one point, the Illinois Central was the largest railroad in the country, with over 700 miles of track in operation. Over time, other railroads became larger, but up until the IC was merged into Canadian National in 1998, it proudly called itself "the Mainline of Mid-America."

At Champaign, another Illinois Central branch line split off from the mainline and headed southwest toward Decatur. This is the depot at White Heath, located about a third of the way between Champaign and Decatur. Built in 1942, the depot was located at another split where a line went due west toward Clinton. Today, the building is abandoned, but the tracks in front of it are owned by the Monticello Railway Museum.

The Cisco depot was built in 1873. Today, the tracks in front of it are owned by the Decatur Central Railroad—a relatively new company that brings grain cars to the Cisco elevator, loads them, and then brings them to Decatur for shipment on larger railroads. The depot sat abandoned for several years, but it is now home to a model railroad club.

This photograph, which was taken on an unknown date, shows an Illinois Central train at the depot in Sabina, near Le Roy. Sabina was located on an IC branch line known as the Punkin Vine, which was originally the Havana, Rantoul & Eastern Railroad but merged into the IC in 1886. The Punkin Vine was abandoned in 1980. (Photograph by Otho Covert; courtesy of Jack Keefe.)

Five

Depots of the Illinois Traction

In 1896, William B. McKinley started the Illinois Traction (IT) System, an electric light rail (or interurban) system that connected various Central Illinois communities with St. Louis. This building is the Peoria depot on the Illinois Traction, which was located on Adams Street. The depot is now used for municipal purposes, but many of its features remain, including the clock tower and interior wooden floors.

This undated photograph shows the back of the Peoria depot. The tracks ran underneath the building, similar to those of other railroads at large union stations around the country. In almost all of the towns the Illinois Traction passed through, it ran down the middle of city streets. This was called streetrunning. (Courtesy of the Illinois Traction Society.)

In addition to passenger service, the Illinois Traction also provided freight service with big, unusual-looking electric locomotives. This is a Class C locomotive leading a freight train past the tiny depot at Gardena just east of Peoria. Today, this portion of the line is a bike path, and a restored Illinois Traction signal is on display at this location. (Courtesy of the Illinois Traction Society.)

The Morton depot was built around 1906. This 1953 photograph shows the depot in its final years of service. Due to increasing competition with automobiles, most interurbans shut down in the 1950s and 1960s. This portion of the Illinois Traction lost passenger service in 1956, and while freight trains hung on until the 1970s, not much remains of the IT in Morton today. (Courtesy of the Illinois Traction Society.)

The Illinois Traction split at Mackinaw Junction. One line went east toward Bloomington and Decatur, and the other went due south toward Lincoln and Springfield. This was the unique depot at the junction as it appeared in 1952. In early 1953, the Bloomington line was abandoned, and the Springfield-to-Peoria segment was abandoned in 1977 following a derailment. (Courtesy of the Illinois Traction Society.)

Just east of Mackinaw Junction is the town of Mackinaw, where this 1910 depot stands on the Bloomington Line. This 1953 photograph shows the depot shortly after the tracks were removed. The tower in the middle of the building was used as a substation for generating and distributing electricity to the overhead wires that powered the trains. The holes in the wall are where the wires came out of the substation, and those connected to the wires that were over the tracks. After the railroad stopped using the structure, it was used by the Illinois Power & Light Company for generating electricity to power the Mackinaw area. (Courtesy of the Illinois Traction Society.)

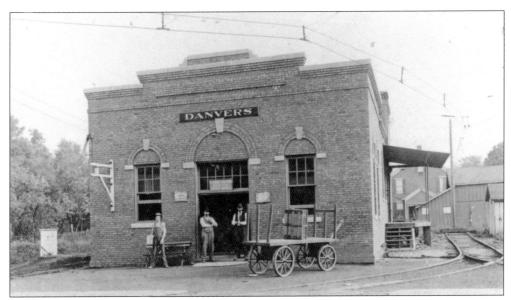

East of Mackinaw, trains on the Illinois Traction stopped at this depot built in 1906 in Danvers. This early photograph shows the depot likely sometime soon after it was placed into service. The cart in front of the depot was used for carrying baggage and mail to and from the trains. Many depots of the era had carts like this; today, they are highly sought-after collectibles for railroad fans. (Courtesy of the Illinois Traction Society.)

The Illinois Traction erected this building on Madison Street in Bloomington to serve as a freight depot, but in 1941, operations from the nearby passenger depot were moved to this building. After the IT abandoned this line in 1953, the building became a warehouse for the Capodice & Sons Produce Company; this building was torn down in 2014. (Courtesy of the McLean County Museum of History.)

This 1941 photograph shows the ticket window inside the Illinois Traction's Bloomington depot. The ticket window reportedly was still intact when the building was torn down in 2014—60 years after it was last used. Passengers Don O'Connor (left) and Robert Harmon are standing in front of the ticket window, and the man behind the ticket window is unidentified. (Courtesy of the McLean County Museum of History.)

The Heyworth depot was built around 1906. It was located at the corner of Main and Walnut Streets in Heyworth and was razed in the early 1960s to make way for an apartment complex. A step leading up to one of the doors of the depot remained in place for many years after the depot was razed. (Courtesy of the Illinois Traction Society.)

One of the Illinois Traction depots that stood for decades after interurban service ended was at Wapella. There were only three depots on the entire railroad with this design (the other two were at Monticello and Girard). The Wapella depot, which was repurposed as a feed storage building, survived a violent 1968 tornado and remained standing until 1999, when it was finally razed. (Courtesy of the Illinois Traction Society.)

At Clinton, the Illinois Traction had this station building that is similar to the one in Danvers. This 1910 photograph likely shows the depot around the time it was built. After the tracks were abandoned in 1953, the depot was sold and had additions built around it on all four sides. Decades later, the depot and the additions were torn down. During the demolition, the additions were removed first, so for a short time, people could catch one last glimpse of the original depot building. (Courtesy of the Illinois Traction Society.)

While the Mackinaw-to-Decatur line of the Illinois Traction was abandoned in 1953, a small portion running between Decatur and Forsyth remained for a short time and provided limited passenger service into Decatur to connect with other lines. This photograph shows a car at the Forsyth depot in the last months of interurban service there. At the time, passenger ridership was so low that the depot building was no longer needed. It was boarded up, and after the Illinois Traction finally got rid of this small operation in 1954, the depot was torn down. (Courtesy of the Illinois Traction Society.)

The Illinois Traction's Decatur depot is located on Van Dyke Street and is now home to a church. This undated photograph shows the depot before the tracks were removed. To this day, one can find rails still in place in the church parking lot. Decatur is where the IT split and headed west to Springfield and east to Danville. (Courtesy of the Illinois Traction Society.)

Decatur was home to the Illinois Traction's main shop facilities where equipment was built, maintained, and repaired. The shops have not been used by any railroad since the 1950s, but several buildings from the complex are still standing. This is a photograph of the storeroom. The little oval near the center of the top of the building is the Illinois Traction System logo.

In downtown Decatur, the Illinois Traction used a former streetcar station known as the Transfer House. Over the years, the Transfer House became a Decatur icon, and in the 1960s, it was relocated to a city park and preserved. Today, it stands as a monument to Decatur's past. This early-1900s photograph shows the Transfer House with trolley cars in the background. (Courtesy of the Illinois Traction Society.)

Moving west from Decatur, one comes to Harristown, where another substation/depot stood to provide electricity for trains. Built in 1910, the Harristown depot was in its final years of service at the time this 1953 photograph was taken. The tracks were removed in 1956, but the depot was repurposed as a business. (Courtesy of the Illinois Traction Society.)

In Illiopolis, the Illinois Traction had another early substation/depot with a design similar to that of the depots at Heyworth and Danvers. This early-1900s view shows an interurban car making a stop at the depot. During World War II, Illiopolis was home to an ammunition factory that was served by the IT and the Wabash Railroad. (Courtesy of the Illinois Traction Society.)

The Illinois Traction's Springfield depot was built around 1910 and razed in 2015. This building was similar in design to the Decatur shop buildings. This March 12, 1955, photograph shows the Springfield depot about a year before passenger service ended. From Springfield, the tracks went south to St. Louis and north to Lincoln and Peoria. (Courtesy of the Illinois Traction Society.)

The Lincoln depot was originally a hotel but was later converted for use as an Illinois Traction station. This was another location on the IT where the tracks ran down the center of the streets. Streetrunning was used by many railroads, but it is rare in modern times due to the many dangers related to running a train down a city street.

There are at least three known communities in Illinois that are named Union. This is one of them, a small hamlet located about halfway between Lincoln and Mackinaw Junction. At one time, Union was home to a general store, grain elevator, church, and armory in addition to this substation depot. (Courtesy of the Illinois Traction Society.)

Near the east end of the Illinois Traction is this depot at Champaign, which the IT once shared with the Wabash Railroad. This 1950s photograph shows an interurban car making a stop at the jointly owned depot. This facility was known as the Belt Depot. The main IT depot in Champaign was located in a downtown storefront building. (Courtesy of the Illinois Traction Society.)

The main Illinois Traction depot in Champaign was located on University Street near the Illinois Central station. The building is still standing and now houses a business. Other than the depot, there are no remaining traces of the IT in this area of Champaign. The city recently redeveloped the area around the IC depot and named it Illinois Terminal Station to honor the interurban.

The Monticello depot was built in 1910. Located at the corner of Market and Livingston Streets in downtown Monticello, this depot was razed in the early 1960s. Passenger service ended through Monticello in 1956, but the railroad continued to be used by freight trains for a few more years. The line was finally abandoned due to extremely tight curves in the downtown Monticello area that were proving to be too difficult for newer locomotives to handle. Today, while most of the Illinois Traction's Monticello-area line is long gone, a small portion remains north of Monticello and sees limited use by the Monticello Railway Museum. (Courtesy of the Illinois Traction Society.)

Six

DEPOTS OF THE WABASH

The Wabash Railroad was one of the major railroads to pass through Central Illinois. Two main lines connected Chicago with Decatur and points east and west. This is the station at Saunemin on the mainline to Chicago. This depot was built in the 1880s and torn down prior to 1975. (Photograph by Jack Keefe.)

The Wabash's depot at Forrest was located at a junction with the Toledo, Peoria & Western. Built in 1893 to replace an earlier depot that was destroyed by fire, the building was once much larger than it is in this 1961 photograph. More fires occurred over the years, which resulted in the building being shortened in length several times. In its heyday, the depot was such a bustling place that a restaurant was opened inside, and a hotel was built nearby for train crews and passengers. Across the tracks, the Wabash operated a small yard and locomotive facility until the early 1930s, when operations were moved to Decatur. (Photograph by Jack Keefe.)

The Wabash depot at Gibson City was built in the 1890s and razed in the 1960s. Today, the site is occupied by a shop for the Bloomer Line, a local short line that collects grain cars from various nearby elevators and brings them to larger railroads in Gibson City for transportation to points across the country. (Photograph by Jack Keefe.)

Until World War II, the depot at Mansfield was an L-shaped building that the Wabash shared with the Peoria & Eastern (P&E) Railroad. In this 1965 photograph, the P&E section had been removed, and the remaining section of the structure was used only by the Wabash. This depot was torn down in 1980. (Photograph by Jack Keefe.)

The Monticello depot was built in 1899 to replace a smaller depot that was destroyed by a fire. In 1904, the tracks through Monticello were relocated, and the depot was moved with them. This 1969 photograph shows the depot at the new location. Today, the tracks are used by the Norfolk Southern Railway. (Photograph by Jack Keefe.)

This 1903 photograph shows the Wabash's 1880 depot at Milmine, south of Monticello. Note the Illinois Traction interurban cars passing in the background. Sometime after this photograph was taken, the depot at Bement burned down, and the Milmine depot was moved there to replace it.

By the time this photograph was taken in 1969, the former Milmine depot—which was now at Bement—had been extensively remodeled both inside and outside. Bement is located at a junction with the Chicago mainline and the Wabash's main east–west corridor. Today, this building is still here, but it has been modified to a point at which it no longer looks like a depot. (Photograph by Jack Keefe.)

The Wabash depot at Decatur was built in 1901. The upper floors were used for offices for railroad staff. In 1964, the Wabash was merged into the Norfolk & Western (N&W) Railway, but the N&W continued to use the building for years. Today, it houses an antique mall. (Photograph by Jack Keefe.)

The Illiopolis Wabash depot was looking a little worse for the wear in this 1960s photograph. Illiopolis was one of the last Wabash depots of this design in the area, and it was demolished soon after this picture was taken. Today, there are no surviving Wabash depots on this portion of the line between Decatur and Springfield. (Courtesy of the Chatham Railroad Museum.)

The Wabash tracks through Springfield were originally owned by the Great Western Railway. This is the former Great Western depot in Springfield, which later became the Wabash depot. In 1861, Abraham Lincoln boarded a train to Washington, DC, here after winning the presidential election. On this platform, he gave his famous farewell speech.

Seven

DEPOTS OF THE CHICAGO & ILLINOIS MIDLAND

The Chicago & Illinois Midland (C&IM) Railroad ran from Taylorville to Peoria. Its primary purpose was to transport coal from mines to power plants in the Peoria area, but it also handled passengers for many years. This was the C&IM's depot built in 1909 at Pekin. The depot was built without a bay window for the agent, which was unusual for stations at the time.

In the small town of Forest City, south of Pekin, is a newer Chicago & Illinois Midland (C&IM) depot from 1949. This building only saw a few years of passenger service, as the C&IM quit running passenger trains in 1953. However, it remained open as a freight agency for years. Today, these tracks are owned by the Illinois & Midland Railway.

The Petersburg depot was one of the most attractive structures on the railroad. The Chicago & Illinois Midland did not replace this structure with a modern one during the 1940s, and it remained standing until the 1960s, when it was razed. This photograph shows a C&IM passenger train making a stop at the Petersburg depot on an unknown date. (Courtesy of the Chatham Railroad Museum.)

The Chicago & Illinois Midland (C&IM) operated a shop complex in Springfield. This depot was located near the shops and a junction with the Wabash Railroad. After passenger train service ended here, the building was used for offices for a time, but by the late 1990s, it had been vacated and boarded up. It was torn down in 2003. (Courtesy of the Chatham Railroad Museum.)

This photograph from the early 1950s shows a Chicago & Illinois Midland steam locomotive at Springfield. No. 502 was a 4-4-0 locomotive and was used to pull the C&IM's last passenger trains. The 4-4-0 was a 19th-century locomotive design, and the C&IM was the last railroad in the country to order them. No. 502 was retired after passenger service ended, and it was subsequently scrapped.

RAIL ROAD DEPOT   PAWNEE ILL.   H.H.BREGSTONE ST.LOUIS

The Pawnee depot was built in 1913 to replace a smaller wooden structure. The previous depot was dismantled and reassembled at Taylorville. This early postcard shows the new depot in Pawnee, likely around the time it was built. After passenger trains stopped running in 1953, the Pawnee depot was closed. Despite efforts from the community to repurpose the depot building, the railroad knocked it down in the early 1960s. However, a smaller brick depot similar to the one in Forest City (see page 70) was built at a small hamlet known as Ellis, a couple of miles outside of Pawnee. That building is still standing today. Bricks and signage from the 1913 Pawnee depot were saved and survive in the collections of local railroad and history buffs. Today, this section of the Chicago & Illinois Midland is hardly used, but one can see the occasional train bringing coal to local power plants. (Courtesy of the Chatham Railroad Museum.)

Eight

DEPOTS OF THE NICKEL PLATE AND PEORIA & EASTERN

Two railroads that paralleled each other from Peoria to points in Indiana were the Nickel Plate Road (NKP) and Peoria & Eastern (P&E) Railway. This 1968 photograph shows the NKP depot at Congerville, east of Peoria. This part of the NKP was originally owned by the Lake Erie & Western Railway, which was acquired by the NKP in 1922. (Photograph by Jack Keefe.)

A few miles southwest of Congerville is the town of Tremont, where the Peoria & Eastern (P&E) built this depot around 1900. This was a common design for P&E structures of the time, and a near-copy of this depot stood at Fithian, Illinois, east of Champaign. Today, Tremont is one of only two P&E depots still standing in the state.

The Peoria & Eastern's depot in Mackinaw was built around 1890. In 1957, the P&E discontinued all passenger trains on this portion of the line. Harvey Gose, the Mackinaw station agent, was able to keep his job for a little over a year until the P&E finally closed the Mackinaw agency. (Photograph by Jack Keefe.)

The village of Danvers was home to this Peoria & Eastern (P&E) depot, which was likely built around 1890, much like the one in Mackinaw. By the time this 1965 photograph was taken, the depot had been out of service for about seven years, and the building had been torn down by 1970. Today, little evidence of the railroad remains in Danvers, as the P&E was abandoned through town in the 1980s. (Photograph by Jack Keefe.)

On the far west side of Bloomington, the Nickel Plate (NKP) and P&E joined each other and ran side-by-side through town. Just south of downtown Bloomington was this depot built by the P&E but also used by the NKP. While trains from both railroads stopped at the Bloomington Union Depot a few blocks away, until 1957, this station was also a scheduled stop.

East of Bloomington, the Peoria & Eastern (P&E) went southeast toward Champaign-Urbana, and the Nickel Plate went due east toward Frankfort, Indiana. The P&E's depot at Le Roy was built in 1913 at a cost of $10,000. Originally, a small, worn-out wooden depot stood here, but after pressuring the railroad for many months, the town finally got a new brick structure. At the time of this 1965 photograph, the Le Roy depot had been sold and repurposed as a business. It was later torn down, but a plaque honoring the town's railroad history was put in its place a few years later. Today, little evidence of the railroad remains in Le Roy. (Photograph by Jack Keefe.)

The Peoria & Eastern was abandoned east of Bloomington in 1994 due to a bridge in Farmer City that needed extensive repairs that the railroad did not want to pay for. The line was largely unused by that point. Shortly after the trains stopped running, the Farmer City depot was razed. This 1963 photograph shows the depot when it was still in service. (Photograph by Jack Keefe.)

The Nickel Plate (NKP) depot at Gibson City lost passenger service on May 1, 1971, when Amtrak took over all passenger trains in the country. The NKP line had low ridership on its trains, so Amtrak did not include the line in its system. However, the depot was turned into an office building for railroad maintenance personnel and still stands today.

Just east of Gibson City is the small village of Elliott, where this depot once stood. Built by the Lake Erie & Western in 1916, the Elliott station closed in the 1950s. Rollie Siebring was the final agent here. During the building's demolition in 1971, the *Gibson City Courier* ran a story about the depot's history titled "Death of a Depot." (Photograph by Jack Keefe.)

The Rankin depot was also built around 1916. Until the 1940s, the Lake Erie & Western and the Nickel Plate operated a large rail yard and shop complex east of town. During World War II, declining rail traffic eliminated the need for a shop complex, and the buildings were torn down. (Photograph by Jack Keefe.)

Nine

UNION DEPOTS AND INTERLOCKING TOWERS

Bloomington-Normal was once home to multiple rail junctions that had depots shared by multiple railroads. Known as union or joint-agency depots, these buildings could be found at almost every junction prior to the 1950s. Built in 1924, the Normal depot was shared by the Chicago & Alton and Illinois Central Railroads. (Photograph by Jack Keefe.)

Opened on October 2, 1913, the Bloomington Union Depot was, at one time, perhaps the busiest building in the city (other than the government buildings downtown). Here, passengers could board north- or southbound trains on the Chicago & Alton/Gulf, Mobile & Ohio route or east- or westbound trains on the Nickel Plate or Peoria & Eastern. The two upper floors of the depot housed offices for railroad personnel as well as a dispatching center. During the wartime periods in the 20th century, Union Depot was where thousands of soldiers said goodbye to their loved ones and, when the wars ended, came home to them. This 1980s photograph shows the depot in its final years of service.

Bloomington Union Depot was the site of many whistle stops on presidential campaign tours. Presidential candidates would travel on trains and stop at various depots to give speeches. Notable candidates who stopped in Bloomington over the years include Franklin Roosevelt, Harry Truman, and Gerald Ford. This 1940 photograph shows a crowd at the depot watching a speech by candidate Wendell Willkie. (Courtesy of the McLean County Museum of History.)

This photograph shows a northbound Amtrak train making a stop at union depot in Bloomington. While the Nickel Plate and Peoria & Eastern discontinued passenger trains in the 1950s, the Gulf, Mobile & Ohio continued operations and eventually handed them over to Amtrak. Today, Amtrak still runs trains on this route. The small building at right is the BN target box, from which an operator dictated train movements across the junction. (Photograph by Steve Smedley.)

In 1990, Amtrak moved its Bloomington-Normal station stop to Normal, and the old union depot was boarded up. This 1990s photograph shows a train passing the abandoned depot and collecting train orders from the BN target operator. The device he is holding is called a train order stick; the conductor or engineer of a passing train would grab the orders from the stick as the train passed. (Photograph by Steve Smedley.)

Interlocking towers were just as important as railroad depots. These interesting structures housed a set of levers that could be pulled to direct trains down different tracks and signal controls to direct train movements through junctions to prevent collisions. This is Dean Tower, which was once located on the south side of Bloomington at the junction of the Illinois Central, Nickel Plate, and Peoria & Eastern. (Photograph by Jack Keefe.)

Edward L. "Eddie" French was one of the operators at Dean Tower in the 1960s. This photograph shows him working the levers inside the tower that directed trains down different tracks. Sometimes depots were equipped with these levers too, but they were mostly found in towers. French later moved to Woodstock, Illinois, and became a teacher. (Courtesy of the McLean County Museum of History.)

Dean Tower was built around 1905 and razed in 1983, shortly after this photograph was taken. By the 1960s, newer interlocking technology was being introduced, and instead of having operators manually control junctions from towers, railroads had a single operator who could control multiple junctions from an office hundreds of miles away. Known as centralized traffic control (CTC), this new technology has made interlocking towers nearly extinct today. (Photograph by Roger A. Holmes.)

Another Illinois Central and Peoria & Eastern interlocking tower stood at Farmer City. Unlike Dean Tower, this tower remained in service into the early 1990s but was eventually closed and demolished. After the 1994 abandonment of the P&E, almost all traces of a junction in Farmer City disappeared. Today, the former Illinois Central line sees several trains per day. (Photograph by Jack Keefe.)

The Chenoa depot was quickly built in 1918 to replace an earlier wood-frame structure that was destroyed by a fire rumored to have been started by a firework from the celebrations at the end of World War I. Located at the junction of the Chicago & Alton and Toledo, Peoria & Western, this station was razed in 2009. (Photograph by Jack Keefe.)

The Toledo, Peoria & Western and Illinois Central built this freight depot in El Paso in 1899. The passenger station was originally located in a nearby hotel, but by the 1920s, the passenger operations had been consolidated into this building. In 1994, just days before the depot was supposed to be torn down, it was saved and relocated a short distance back from the tracks, where it remains today.

Springfield Union Station opened on January 2, 1898. Although it was used by several railroads, the station was designed and constructed by the Illinois Central. Originally built with a soaring 110-foot clock tower, Springfield Union Station lost much of its architectural character when the tower was removed in 1946. The depot was served by the Illinois Central, Chicago & Illinois Midland and Baltimore & Ohio, as well as the predecessors of those railroads. The depot was not near any rail lines, so tracks were built down the center of the adjacent street. When the depot was closed in 1971, the tracks were paved over and are rumored to still be in place under the pavement. (Photograph by Jack Keefe.)

Springfield was once home to several interlocking towers that were located throughout the city at various rail junctions. This 1990 photograph shows a northbound Amtrak Train passing Ridgely Tower, which was built around 1910 and razed in 2011. This was the last of the Springfield towers utilized in active service. (Photograph by Steve Smedley.)

Iles Tower, built around 1900, was located on the south side of Springfield at a junction between the Chicago & Alton and the Wabash. This 1940s photograph shows a steam train passing Iles Tower on the C&A line. In the 1990s, the tower was removed and the junction was rebuilt. (Courtesy of the Chatham Railroad Museum.)

Starnes, another Wabash tower in Springfield, was located at a junction between the Wabash, Illinois Central, and Illinois Traction System. At many towers throughout the area, the operators would take up hobbies to keep themselves busy during the time in between trains that they had to manage. Most played cards or read books, and some even took up hunting if the tower was located in a rural area. The operators at Starnes spent their free time planting and maintaining a garden across the tracks from the tower building. Over the years, interest waned in the garden, and nature slowly reclaimed it during the 1960s and 1970s. (Photograph by Jack Keefe.)

Springfield's Avenue Tower was one of the busiest in the area. It controlled a junction between the Illinois Central (IC), Chicago & Illinois Midland (C&IM), Chicago & Alton, and Baltimore & Ohio Railroads. Avenue Tower was designed and built by the IC around 1900 and shared the design of other IC towers. Avenue Tower closed in November 1992 and was torn down a few months later. (Photograph by Steve Smedley.)

Shops Tower was a few blocks from Avenue Tower at a junction with the C&IM and Wabash Railroads. The C&IM's Springfield depot was located near here. Shops Tower is the last interlocking tower still standing in Springfield and the last surviving C&IM tower, although it is boarded up and vacant.

TY Tower in Tuscola controlled a junction between the Illinois Central, Chicago & Eastern Illinois, and Baltimore & Ohio railroads. It was built in 1899 and torn down in 1994. The railroads offered to sell it to Tuscola for preservation for $1, but the town declined and instead built a replica tower in a park. (Photograph by Jack Keefe.)

This 1990 photograph shows a CSX freight train passing TY Tower on the former Baltimore & Ohio (B&O) line. The B&O was merged into the CSX Transportation System in 1987. The former Chicago & Eastern Illinois line is now operated by the Union Pacific, and the Illinois Central is now operated by the Canadian National Railway. (Photograph by Steve Smedley.)

At Paxton, Illinois, the Illinois Central (IC) line crossed that of the Lake Erie & Western (LE&W). The IC tracks passed beneath the LE&W in a cut through the center of town. The Paxton depot was built at the LE&W overpass and located at the same level as the LE&W tracks, with stairs going down to the IC tracks. This depot was demolished in the mid-1970s. (Photograph by Jack Keefe.)

The Hoopeston depot was located at a junction between the Lake Erie & Western and Chicago & Eastern Illinois lines. The building was of a highly unusual design and was the only depot of its type in the area. Hoopeston was a popular place for railfans to take pictures of trains, and this depot is visible in the backgrounds of many photographs from Hoopeston. Unfortunately, despite efforts to preserve the building, it was torn down in the early 1980s. (Photograph by Jack Keefe.)

Moving farther north on the Illinois Central to the village of Ashkum, one will see this interlocking tower that was built in the 1920s. While most towers were located at junctions between two railroads, Ashkum Tower was located on a single Illinois Central mainline to control train movements on the often-congested IC. When centralized traffic control was put into service in the 1950s, Ashkum Tower was closed. However, the building remains standing and now houses equipment for railroad maintenance workers.

Ten

CENTRAL ILLINOIS DEPOTS TODAY

During the 1970s, a number of communities preserved their depots for use as community centers, businesses, museums, and even fire and police stations. One of the first towns to preserve its depot for community use was Roanoke, which moved and restored its 1896 Santa Fe depot in 1974. Today, the building houses an art museum and is the only preserved Santa Fe depot in the area.

In 1971, the Wabash depot from Sibley was sold into private ownership and moved back from the tracks. It was built in 1880 and damaged in a 1903 fire that resulted in a large portion of the building being removed. Over the years, it has had various uses, but today is home to a photography studio. The owner is slowly but surely working on restoring the building to how it appeared in the early 1900s. It is hoped that someday a caboose can be acquired and placed on display out front. Several other local depot restoration projects have used measurements taken from various parts of the Sibley depot to use in their projects.

For the bicentennial celebrations of 1975 and 1976, the village of Bellflower purchased its Illinois Central depot from the railroad and moved it to the town park for restoration. Work was completed by July 1976, and since then, the town has held many events at the depot. Bellflower was originally spelled "Belleflower," and during the restoration of the depot, that spelling of the name was painted on one of the town name signs that are on each end of the building ("Bellflower" is on the other sign). Today, the depot is maintained by the Bellflower Historical Society and home to a town museum that is open every Fourth of July or by appointment.

In 2005, Springfield Union Station was restored. The clock tower, which was removed in 1946, was reconstructed, and the interior was restored to its 1930s appearance. At first, it was used as a visitors' center for the nearby Abraham Lincoln Presidential Museum, but in 2018–2019, it was turned into a railroad museum to house exhibits highlighting Springfield's railroading history.

In May 2019, the Iowa Interstate Railroad brought one of its vintage steam locomotives to Chillicothe to pull railfan excursions that raised money for local fire departments. The restored Rock Island depot was the starting point of the excursion trips. This was the first steam locomotive to stop at the Chillicothe depot since the 1950s, when the Rock Island switched to diesel power.

During the summer of 1971, the Chicago & Alton depot from Shirley was sold to Robert Rehtmeyer. Rehtmeyer loaded the depot onto a truck and transported it to his property in Funks Grove. After it had been moved, the building was restored and slightly modified for use as an antique store. Changes to the building included the removal of the door to the baggage room and the addition of a couple of windows. After a few years, the antique store closed, and the building has been used for storage since then. The Shirley depot is not in the best shape today, but the owners are doing their best to keep it looking presentable.

Many of the former Illinois Traction interurban depots were torn down in the 1960s. However, several were preserved. The Harristown depot was rescued and restored. It was turned into a commercial space and has housed many businesses over the years. In the 1980s, the body of a retired interurban car was put on display in front of the depot. By the early 2010s, the property was in bad shape, so the owners began—and are still in the process of—repairing and sprucing up the depot. At the time of this writing in late 2020, the interurban car is for sale. (Photograph by Isaiah Bradford.)

From the 1980s until the early 2010s, the Wabash depot at Forrest stood abandoned and in disrepair. The Forrest Historical Society (FHS) spent many hours restoring the structure to its original appearance for use as a railroad museum. In addition to restoring the depot, the FHS also restored a nearby turntable—a device used to turn around locomotives to direct them down different tracks—that was from the pre–World War II era of steam locomotives. The museum opened in late 2014 and is currently open several times throughout the year for the public to enjoy.

In 1980, the Wabash depot at Monticello was relocated to a site along the former Illinois Central tracks. The IC line is owned by the Monticello Railway Museum, and the Wabash depot was restored for use by the museum. Today, it serves its original purpose as a train station for the museum's excursion trains, which feature historic locomotives and cars.

Heyworth lost its Illinois Central depot decades ago, but in 2005, a restored Illinois Central caboose was brought to town and placed on display. In 2020, the museum moved the caboose to the site of the depot. The caboose houses several displays of railroad memorabilia, artifacts, and model trains. It is open to the public during several weekends throughout the summer.

Although the Normal depot was torn down in the 1970s, Amtrak has continued to stop in the town at newer facilities. This station was built in 1991 to replace the Bloomington Union Depot. Its closer proximity to Illinois State University greatly increased the number of passengers and allowed for much easier access to trains, since the union depot was in a more remote location. (Photograph by Ryan Tidaback.)

In 2012, the 1991 Amtrak depot was replaced with Uptown Station, a combination train depot, bus depot, and town hall. This depot is equipped with modern features, but the exterior was designed to have a vintage look, including a large clock and brick siding. Uptown Station sits on the site that was once occupied by the original Normal depot. (Photograph by Ryan Tidaback.)

This photograph shows an Amtrak train making a stop at Uptown Station. Currently, 10 Amtrak trains make stops here each day, and the station also sees the occasional passing of a freight train from the Union Pacific. While train activity is nowhere near what it used to be in Normal, the town remains a thriving railroad community. (Photograph by Tyler Scott.)

The Illinois Central depot at Flanagan was built in the 1940s and relocated two blocks from its original location in the 1970s. The town restored the building and currently uses it as a town hall. After the depot in Pontiac was demolished in 2019, the Flanagan depot became the only surviving IC depot on the Pontiac branch line.

Form A

TOLEDO, PEORIA & WESTERN RAILROAD

HISTORICAL SOCIETY MEMBERSHIP SIGN UP CARD

Station _____ Date _____ 20 ___

Name (First & Last) _____

Email Address _____

Reason For Joining _____

Interested in submitting articles and/or photos for the society newsletter?

Yes ☐ No ☐ (If checked YES, you will be contacted about submissions for an upcoming newsletter.)

THANK YOU FOR JOINING THE TP&WHS!

Built in 1900, the Jacksonville depot on the Chicago & Alton's Jacksonville branch line was restored in the 1970s and turned into a restaurant. Today, the depot is immaculately maintained, and the original "Jacksonville" station sign is mounted on the back side of the building. Additionally, the train order signal that once stood trackside has been restored and put on display in the parking lot for the restaurant.

The Lacon Chicago & Alton (C&A) depot is of newer construction and replaced an earlier, much larger wood-frame structure. When the tracks through Lacon were removed in the 1970s, the building was sold into private ownership and heavily modified for use as a restaurant. At one point, the C&A was making plans to build an extension from this line south to Peoria to connect with another one of its lines, but this never happened.

Many villages near Peoria have repurposed their depots. The Chicago, Burlington & Quincy (CB&Q) depot at Canton has been restored and turned into offices for the town. It was built in 1914 and is an example of the CB&Q's "county seat" depot design, which was only used in towns that were county seats. The tracks were abandoned in the early 2000s, but a small portion of track remains in front of the depot. A restored diesel locomotive that once worked in a local mine has been put on display in the parking lot.

In somewhat rare instances, old depots are still in active service. The 1949 Chicago & Illinois Midland depot at Havana is currently being used by the Illinois & Midland Railroad, current owner of the C&IM, for offices and storage. Prior to this depot being built, the C&IM's Havana depot was located downtown, and trains had to run down a city street to reach it. This new depot allowed for much safer conditions surrounding the passing trains.

Another depot still in use is the Chicago, Burlington & Quincy depot at Beardstown. In 1971, the CB&Q was merged into the Burlington Northern, and in 1996, the BN merged with the Santa Fe to form BNSF Railway. BNSF currently operates the former CB&Q line out of Beardstown and uses the depot as a base for maintenance workers and equipment.

While finding preserved depots is rare, finding preserved roundhouses is nearly impossible. Roundhouses were large, circular-shaped sheds used for storing and maintaining locomotives. During the 1950s, they were largely phased out, and due to their large size and often being located in or next to active rail yards, preserving them can be difficult. The Chicago, Burlington & Quincy roundhouse at Beardstown is one of the few survivors and has been restored and turned into a community center. Inside are several exhibits showing the glory days of railroading in Beardstown during the first half of the 20th century.

In the 1960s, the Chicago, Burlington & Quincy relocated its Beardstown line to higher ground to avoid flooding from the adjacent Illinois River. One of the towns that lost rail service as a result was Browning, where this 1870s depot still stands today. After the railroad was relocated, the Browning depot fell into a state of disrepair. Thankfully, during the 1990s, it was cosmetically restored. Today, it is privately owned and used for storage.

The Baltimore & Ohio depot at Virginia, Illinois, was turned into a restaurant many years ago. Recently, the structure sustained serious damage from a fire, but it was rebuilt. The original brick walls from the depot can be seen inside. Besides the depot, very few traces of the railroad remain in Virginia. The Baltimore & Ohio was one of the first railroads in the United States, and today, it is part of the CSX Transportation system.

Moving back east, one will find the small hamlet of McDowell situated southeast of Pontiac on a long-abandoned Wabash branch line. In the early 1930s, this line lost passenger service, and the 1873 McDowell depot was sold to a local farmer. The farmer loaded the depot onto a trailer and used a tractor to pull it to his property just outside of town. Amazingly, 90 years later, the depot is still on the farm, and despite having some minor modifications, it looks nearly the same as it did when it was removed from the railroad property.

The Illinois Central depot from DeLand was moved to the Monticello Railway Museum in 1980. It was built in 1919 and is the last surviving depot from the IC's Clinton-to-White Heath branch line. Currently, the depot is located at a former stop on the Illinois Traction known as Nelson, so the museum made new signs for the depot that say "Nelson's Crossing." The original "DeLand" signs are on display inside the building.

Although the Paxton passenger depot was torn down, the Lake Erie & Western freight depot survives and is home to the Illinois Central Historical Society (ICHS). Inside, multiple exhibits show the history of the Illinois Central Railroad, and outside, a restored IC boxcar and caboose are on display. The ICHS recently gave full control of the museum to the Monticello Railway Museum, which designated this site as its North Campus.

In the early 1990s, the abandoned Peoria & Eastern depot at Tremont was restored and had additions built onto it. Interestingly, the additions were designed to match the depot, and the building is now home to multiple businesses. The Peoria & Eastern tracks through Tremont were abandoned in the 1980s, and besides the depot, only faint traces of the roadbed remain today.

Sometimes, when a town wanted to preserve a piece of its railroad history but there was no depot available, a caboose would be acquired for display instead. The town of Chatsworth, located along the Toledo, Peoria & Western (TP&W), has preserved this former TP&W caboose. The Chatsworth Historical Society maintains it and opens it to the public several times throughout the year.

The Mackinaw Illinois Traction depot is one of the few depots in Central Illinois listed in the National Register of Historic Places. It was added to the register on November 30, 1978. This

greatly assisted with the restoration of the depot in the 1980s. Today, the building is home to a tea room and collectible shop. It is a popular venue for events held by the Illinois Traction Society.

The Peoria & Eastern depot in Urbana was about to be demolished in the 1970s, but it was saved, restored, and turned into a business. Today, it is home to a theater. The former P&E tracks are

currently in use by the Norfolk Southern (NS) Railway, but their time is running out, as NS is planning to abandon them. Once they are abandoned, the right-of-way is set to become a bike path.

Unfortunately, while some depots have been preserved, others are rotting away in the weeds next to the railroads that they once served. One example can be found in the small community of Reading, south of Streator. This Santa Fe depot was built in 1888 and has been used as a hay barn since the 1920s. Hay barns do not require much maintenance, so the depot's condition has rapidly declined over the years.

The Illinois Traction depot at Union has been used for storage since the 1950s and has fallen into a severe state of disrepair. It was built in 1909 and closed in 1956 after passenger service ended. Afterward, it was sold into private ownership. Thankfully, the current owner is working with local railfans to restore the depot to its former glory for use as a museum.

DISCOVER THOUSANDS OF LOCAL HISTORY BOOKS
FEATURING MILLIONS OF VINTAGE IMAGES

Arcadia Publishing, the leading local history publisher in the United States, is committed to making history accessible and meaningful through publishing books that celebrate and preserve the heritage of America's people and places.

Find more books like this at
www.arcadiapublishing.com

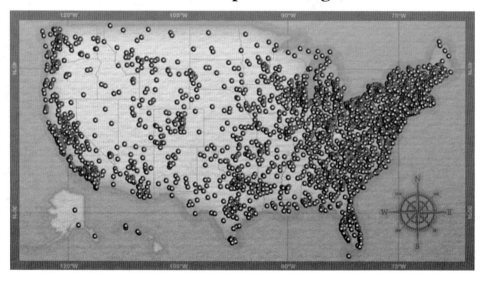

Search for your hometown history, your old stomping grounds, and even your favorite sports team.

Consistent with our mission to preserve history on a local level, this book was printed in South Carolina on American-made paper and manufactured entirely in the United States. Products carrying the accredited Forest Stewardship Council (FSC) label are printed on 100 percent FSC-certified paper.

MADE IN THE USA